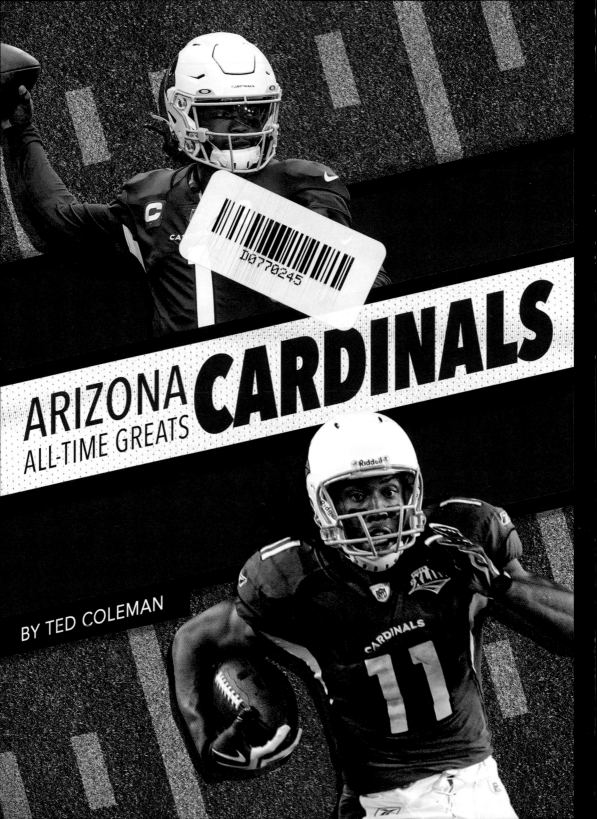

ARIZONA CARDINALS
ALL-TIME GREATS

BY TED COLEMAN

Book design by Jake Slavik
Cover design by Jake Slavik

Photographs ©: Rick Scuteri/AP Images, cover (top), 1 (top); Mark Humphrey/AP Images, cover (bottom), 1 (bottom); Pro Football Hall of Fame/AP Images, 4; AP Images, 7; Vernon Biever/AP Images, 8; David Durochik/AP Images, 10; Al Messerschmidt/AP Images, 13; Greg Trott/AP Images, 14; Ross D. Franklin/AP Images, 17, 21; Ryan Kang/AP Images, 19; Rick Scuteri/AP Images, 20

Press Box Books, an imprint of Press Room Editions.

ISBN
978-1-63494-419-9 (library bound)
978-1-63494-436-6 (paperback)
978-1-63494-469-4 (epub)
978-1-63494-453-3 (hosted ebook)

Library of Congress Control Number: 2021916389

Distributed by North Star Editions, Inc.
2297 Waters Drive
Mendota Heights, MN 55120
www.northstareditions.com

Printed in the United States of America
012022

ABOUT THE AUTHOR

Ted Coleman is a sportswriter who lives in Louisville, Kentucky, with his trusty Affenpinscher, Chloe.

TABLE OF CONTENTS

NEVERS
11

CHAPTER 1
THE CHICAGO YEARS

The Arizona Cardinals are the oldest team in the National Football League (NFL). Their history dates back to 1898. At that time, the Cardinals were an amateur team in Chicago, Illinois. In 1920, the Chicago Cardinals joined a professional league. That league soon became known as the NFL.

The Cardinals had some of the biggest stars of pro football's early days. **John "Paddy" Driscoll** played quarterback, kicked, and even coached. **Ernie Nevers** could do it all, too. In one game against the rival Chicago Bears, Nevers scored every single point for his team.

He had six rushing touchdowns and kicked four extra points.

Marshall Goldberg played multiple roles, too. He ran the ball on offense, played good defense, and returned kicks. Goldberg was a key member of the 1947 Cardinals. That team won the NFL title.

Running back **Ollie Matson** was an excellent rusher. He had been a sprinter in college. He also won two medals at the 1952 Olympics. As a Cardinal, he rushed for 24 touchdowns. But Matson was a

THE MILLION DOLLAR BACKFIELD

The Cardinals didn't do much winning in their early years. But that changed in the 1940s thanks to the "Million Dollar Backfield." Quarterback **Paul Christman** led the group. He was joined by running backs **Pat Harder**, **Elmer Angsman**, and **Charley Trippi**. These offensive weapons led Chicago to the 1947 NFL championship.

MATSON
33

great receiver, too. He hauled in 16 touchdown catches during his time with Chicago.

But Chicago's biggest star was cornerback **Dick "Night Train" Lane.** Lane was a fearsome hitter. Few offensive players could escape him. Lane played for the Cardinals from 1954 to 1959.

WILSON
8

CHAPTER 2
THE ST. LOUIS YEARS

In the 1960 NFL Draft, the Cardinals selected safety **Larry Wilson**. By the time Wilson played that fall, the team had moved to St. Louis, Missouri. Wilson made eight Pro Bowls as a Cardinal. He also set the team record for most interceptions. Wilson was loyal to the Cardinals for decades. He worked as a coach and in the team's front office until 2003.

Jim Hart served as quarterback for most of the team's time in St. Louis. Hart's strong arm kept the Cardinals in games for 17 seasons. In 1974 and 1975, he led the Cardinals to their only division titles in St. Louis.

SMITH
81

One of Hart's top weapons was tight end
Jackie Smith. Smith was a talented blocker.
But he was also a great receiver with blazing

speed. Smith made a name for himself as a reliable target. He recorded at least one catch in 45 straight games from 1967 to 1970. When Smith retired, he was the NFL's all-time leading tight end in catches, yards, and receiving touchdowns.

Cornerback **Roger Wehrli** roamed the secondary alongside Larry Wilson. Wehrli was a Missouri native. He made seven Pro Bowls in the 1970s. If quarterbacks dared throw his way, Wehrli often ended up with the ball. Wehrli notched 40 career interceptions. He also had a team-record 19 fumble recoveries.

STAT SPOTLIGHT

CAREER PASSING TOUCHDOWNS
CARDINALS TEAM RECORD
Jim Hart: 209

Offensive lineman **Dan Dierdorf** helped keep defenders out of the quarterback's face. Dierdorf played his entire career in St. Louis. He was a six-time Pro Bowler and later became a broadcaster.

Dierdorf also opened holes for running back **Ottis Anderson**. Anderson rushed for more than 1,000 yards in five of his first six seasons. By the time he left the Cardinals in 1986, he was the team's all-time rushing leader.

Wide receiver **Roy Green** was another offensive star. The Cardinals struggled in the 1980s, but Green was one of the team's

AIR CORYELL

Cardinals head coach **Don Coryell** revolutionized the NFL. His high-flying passing offense became known as "Air Coryell." Coryell used this offense to great success with the San Diego Chargers in the 1980s. But he first used the offense as the coach in St. Louis. Coryell led the Cardinals for five seasons. During that time, the team won back-to-back division titles.

ANDERSON
32

bright spots. When Green left the Cardinals after the 1990 season, he had the most receiving yards in team history.

WILLIAMS
35

CHAPTER 3
THE ARIZONA YEARS

The Cardinals moved again in 1988. This time, they headed to Arizona. One of their biggest stars at the time was **Freddie Joe Nunn**. Nunn played both linebacker and defensive end. He went on to become the team's all-time leader in sacks.

The Cardinals defense changed forever when the team drafted defensive back **Aeneas Williams** in 1991. Williams was durable, dependable, and one of the hardest hitters in the league. In the 1998 season, Williams grabbed two interceptions in a playoff game.

He helped the team earn its first playoff win since 1947.

Safety **Adrian Wilson** was a great defender in coverage. He could also rush the quarterback. Wilson became just the sixth player in history to record 25 career interceptions and 25 career sacks. Wilson was also a team captain. He retired after the 2012 season and later worked in the team's front office.

Wide receiver **Larry Fitzgerald Jr.** rewrote the Cardinals record book. He arrived in 2004 and quickly became one of the NFL's greatest

STAT SPOTLIGHT

CAREER RECEIVING YARDS
CARDINALS TEAM RECORD
Larry Fitzgerald Jr.: 17,492

FITZGERALD
11

receivers. Only Jerry Rice of the San Francisco 49ers compiled more receiving yards and catches in his career.

The Cardinals became an NFL powerhouse when **Kurt Warner** joined the team. Warner had already won a Super Bowl when he came to Arizona in 2005. In 2008, he had one of the best passing seasons in team history. Better yet, he led Arizona to the Super Bowl. During that game, Warner threw two of his three touchdowns to Fitzgerald. Unfortunately for Cardinals fans, Arizona lost a close game to the Pittsburgh Steelers.

The Cardinals struggled to bounce back after their Super Bowl loss. The team was still rebuilding when linebacker **Chandler Jones** arrived in 2016. The

PAT TILLMAN
Cardinals defensive back **Pat Tillman** walked away from football in 2002. He decided to join the US Army. Tillman served in Iraq and Afghanistan. In 2004, he was killed in action. The Cardinals honored Tillman's memory by retiring his No. 40 jersey.

JONES
55

next year, he led the NFL in sacks. Jones was
the defensive star the Cardinals needed as they
tried to become winners again.

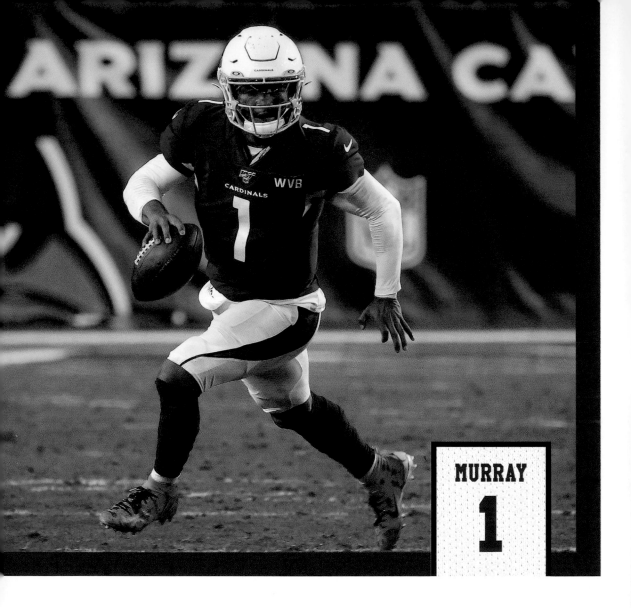

MURRAY

1

The Cardinals had the first pick in the 2019 NFL Draft. They used it on quarterback **Kyler Murray**. Murray was more than just a strong and accurate passer. He was also a speedy runner who could break free at any time. Murray earned Rookie of the Year honors in 2019. And in 2020, he made the Pro Bowl for the first time.

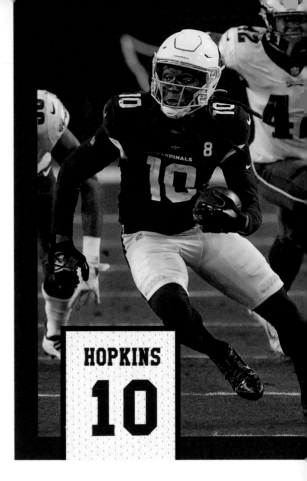

Murray got a big weapon in 2020. That's when Arizona traded for wide receiver **DeAndre Hopkins**. Hopkins had been to the Pro Bowl four times as a member of the Houston Texans. Partnered with Murray, Hopkins exploded for more than 1,400 yards in 2020. Cardinals fans hoped Murray and Hopkins would be the duo to lead Arizona back to the Super Bowl.

TIMELINE

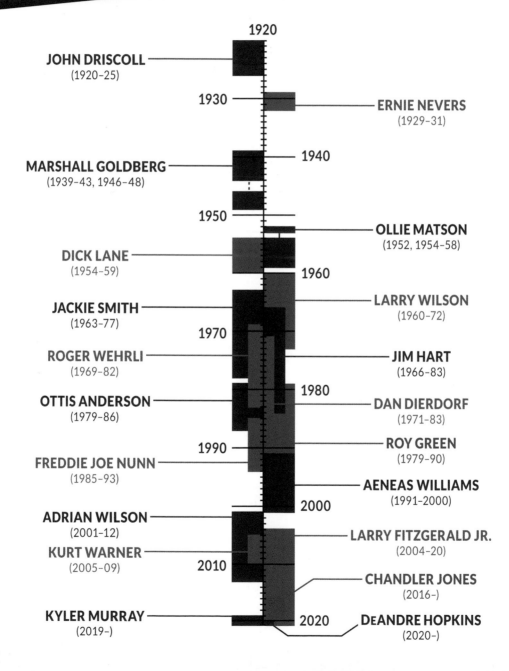

JOHN DRISCOLL
(1920–25)

1920

1930

ERNIE NEVERS
(1929–31)

MARSHALL GOLDBERG
(1939–43, 1946–48)

1940

1950

OLLIE MATSON
(1952, 1954–58)

DICK LANE
(1954–59)

JACKIE SMITH
(1963–77)

1960

LARRY WILSON
(1960–72)

1970

ROGER WEHRLI
(1969–82)

JIM HART
(1966–83)

1980

OTTIS ANDERSON
(1979–86)

DAN DIERDORF
(1971–83)

ROY GREEN
(1979–90)

1990

FREDDIE JOE NUNN
(1985–93)

AENEAS WILLIAMS
(1991–2000)

ADRIAN WILSON
(2001–12)

2000

LARRY FITZGERALD JR.
(2004–20)

KURT WARNER
(2005–09)

2010

CHANDLER JONES
(2016–)

KYLER MURRAY
(2019–)

2020

DEANDRE HOPKINS
(2020–)

ARIZONA CARDINALS

Team history: Chicago Cardinals (1920-43, 1945-59), Chicago/Pittsburgh Cardinals/Steelers (1944), St. Louis Cardinals (1960-87), Phoenix Cardinals (1988-93), Arizona Cardinals (1994-)

NFL championships: 2 (1925, 1947)

Super Bowl titles: 0*

Key coaches:

Jimmy Conzelman (1940-48), 34-31-3, 1 NFL championship

Don Coryell (1973-77), 42-27-1

Ken Whisenhunt (2007-12), 45-51-0

Bruce Arians (2013-17), 49-30-1

MORE INFORMATION

To learn more about the Arizona Cardinals, go to **pressboxbooks.com/AllAccess**.

These links are routinely monitored and updated to provide the most current information available.

1966 through 2020

GLOSSARY

amateur
Having to do with players who are not paid.

cornerback
A defensive player who covers wide receivers near the sidelines.

defensive end
A player who plays on either end of the defensive line and typically rushes the passer.

draft
An event that allows teams to choose new players coming into the league.

linebacker
A player who lines up behind the defensive linemen and in front of the defensive backs.

rookie
A professional athlete in his or her first year of competition.

sack
A tackle of the quarterback behind the line of scrimmage.

secondary
The defensive players who typically cover wide receivers.

INDEX